Abraham's Sacrifice

The Word of the King Series

Abraham's Sacrifice

by

Cor Van Rijswijk

Illustrated by Rino Visser

INHERITANCE PUBLICATIONS
NEERLANDIA, ALBERTA, CANADA
PELLA, IOWA, U.S.A.
ROMSEY, HANTS, UNITED KINGDOM

National Library of Canada Cataloguing in Publication Data
Rijswijk, Cor van, 1939-
  Abraham's sacrifice

  (The word of the King)
  Translation of: Het offer van Abraham.
  ISBN 1-894666-21-6
  1. Abraham (Biblical patriarch)—Juvenile literature. 2. Bible stories,
English. O.T. Genesis. I. Visser, Rino. II. Title. III.
Series: Word of the King.
BS580.A3R54 2001   j222'.11092   C2001-910079-5

Library of Congress Cataloging-in-Publication Data
Rijswijk, Cor van, 1939 -
  [Offer van Abraham. English]
  Abraham's sacrifice / by Cor van Rijswijk ; illustrated by Rino Visser.
    p. cm. — (The word of the King series)
  ISBN 1-894666-21-6
  1. Abraham (Biblical patriarch)— Juvenile literature. 2. Isaac (Biblical
patriarch)—Sacrifice— Juvenile literature. 3. Patriarchs (Bible)—
Biography—Juvenile literature. 4. Bible. O.T. Genesis—Biography—Juvenile
literature. 5. Bible stories—O.T.
  [1. Abraham (Biblical patriarch) 2. Isaac (Biblical patriarch)]
  I. Visser, Rino, ill. II. Title.
BS1238.S24.R5513 2001
222'.1109505—dc21
                                                          2001016646

Originally published as *Het Offer van Abraham* (1997)
by Uitgeverij/Boekhandel Gebr. Koster, Barneveld, The Netherlands
Published with permission.

Translated by Roelof & Theresa Janssen
Cover Painting and Illustrations by Rino Visser

All rights reserved © 2001 by Inheritance Publications
Box 154, Neerlandia, Alberta Canada T0G 1R0
Tel. & Fax (780) 674 3949
Web site: http://www.telusplanet.net/public/inhpubl/webip/ip.htm
E-Mail inhpubl@telusplanet.net

Published simultaneously in U.S.A. by Inheritance Publications
Box 366, Pella, Iowa 50219

Published simultaneously in the United Kingdom by
Inheritance Publications (U.K.) 19 Tench Way, Romsey, Hants, SO51 7RX

Available in Australia from Inheritance Publications
Box 1122, Kelmscott, W.A. 6111 Tel. & Fax (089) 390 4940

Printed in Canada

Contents

Chapter   *Page*

1. A Great Miracle 7
2. The Greatest Treasure 9
3. Look! What Did Abraham Do? 11
4. Later A Child Would Be Born 13
5. Abraham, Count the Stars! 15
6. See, Here I Am 17
7. What Would Abraham Do? 19
8. That Could Not Be Right 21
9. Abraham Loved the Lord 23
10. The Journey 24
11. We Will Come Back 26
12. My Father, Where is the Lamb? 28
13. You Are the Lamb! 32
14. Here I Am, Father! 34
15. Tied Down 36
16. Abraham! Abraham! 38
17. Still An Animal 40
18. The Greatest Miracle 42

1. A Great Miracle

Abraham was rich.
He had many cows and sheep,
donkeys and camels.
He also had lots
of gold and silver.
The LORD had given him
all these animals
and things.

Abraham also had a child.
His name was Isaac.
Oh, Abraham
loved him very much.
He had also received
that child from the LORD.
That had been
a great miracle,
for Abraham and his wife
were already very old.
And old people
do not receive children.
They are much too old
to care for them.
But Abraham and his wife
had received Isaac
from the LORD
while they were old.

No wonder they loved
their only boy very much.
He was a great treasure to them.

2. The Greatest Treasure

Yet, Abraham and his wife
knew greater riches.
They had a greater treasure.
A treasure that could not be lost.
One can lose money.
Whoever is rich today
can be poor tomorrow.
And he who dies
can take nothing along.
Abraham and his wife
knew that very well.
But they had a treasure
they could never lose.
Not even when they died!
Abraham and his wife
feared the Lord.
They loved Him.
He was their greatest riches
and their greatest treasure.

Abraham and his wife
loved their
only son Isaac
very much.
They also loved their servants
and their animals.
But they loved
the Lord most of all.

Of Him they could sing:

*Whom do I have in heav'n but Thee?
Who shall on earth my refuge be?
Since I have Thee as Rock and Saviour,
I seek no further wealth or favour.*[1]

---
[1] Psalm 73:8a in the rhymed version of the
Book of Praise: Anglo-Genevan Psalter.

3. Look! What Did Abraham Do?

Sometimes Abraham
took an animal.
He took it to
a kind of table
and laid the animal on it.
Look at what he did then!
He killed the animal
and then burned it.
Large clouds of smoke
went up on high.

Oh, Abraham
looked very grave
while doing this work.
For he was showing reverence
to the Lord!
He knew that
the Lord wanted
to teach him something
by this sacrificial lamb.
The Lord taught him:
"Abraham,
that animal died
instead of you.
You should have died
for your sins.
But now you may stay alive!"

No wonder
Abraham was very grave;
no wonder
he was very reverent.

Burnt sacrifices I shall offer,
With choicest fatlings pay my vows.
With smoke of rams, with goats and bullocks
I shall adore Thee in Thy house.[2]

---
[2] Psalm 66:6b from the *Book of Praise*.

4. Later A Child Would Be Born

Abraham knew it very well.
The LORD was not satisfied
with this small lamb.
Later the great Lamb
would come.
That Lamb was
the Child of Bethlehem,
the Son of God.
When Abraham
thought of that,
he rejoiced.
He knew
that Child
would come for him.
Yes, that
the Son of God
would even *die* for him.
Because of that death
Abraham
was allowed
to live forever
with the LORD.

Abraham could rejoice:

Thee, holy Lamb of God, we bless.
Thou'st through Thy cross redemption sent us,
And to the Father dost present us
As priests and kings in holiness.[3]

---
[3] Hymn 22a *Book of Praise*

5. Abraham, Count the Stars!

Once the Lord
took Abraham outside.
Oh, it was very dark.
High above
the stars twinkled
like little lights.
"Abraham,
count the stars!"
said the Lord.
"Lord, I cannot do that,"
Abraham answered.
"There are too many!"

Then the Lord
told Abraham
a secret.
"Abraham,
now you only have
one child,
that is Isaac,
your son.
But you will become
the father
of many nations;
a people
so great in number
they cannot be counted.

There will be
poor people
and rich people
in those nations.
But the greatest King
will be
the Child of Bethlehem.
He will come
to save His people.
Abraham,
I have made the stars.
I also will make you
into a great nation.
Do you believe that,
Abraham?"

Yes, Abraham believed
that the Lord
would do all this.
Oh, it made him
very happy.
And he thought
often about the coming
of that Child,
his Saviour!

6. See, Here I Am

On a certain day
Abraham heard
the voice of the Lord.
"Abraham," said the Lord.
Abraham heard His voice.
He knew the voice of
the Good Shepherd.
Many years ago that voice
had also spoken to him.
Then the Lord had said,
"Leave your land
and your friends
and go to a land
which I will show you."
And Abraham had gone
along an unknown
and long way.

He said, "To you this land I give,
That as My heirs you there may live." [4]

---
[4] Psalm 105:4c *Book of Praise*

So Abraham had gone
into the land of the Bible.
By now he had already lived
many years
as a stranger
in the land of the Lord.
The Lord often spoke
with Abraham.
He knew the voice
of the Lord, his God.

Right away Abraham
recognized
the voice of the Lord.
Very reverently
he listened
and responded,
"See, here I am."
What was the Lord
going to say?

7. What Would Abraham Do?

"Abraham,"
said the Lord,
"take your son,
take your only son Isaac,
whom you love so much,
and sacrifice him to Me.
Go to the mountain
to which I will direct you,
and offer him to Me there
as a sacrifice!"

Abraham heard
the voice of the Lord.
The Lord did not ask for an animal.
Neither did the Lord ask for a servant.
No, the Lord asked for his child,
his Isaac.

And it was exactly this boy
whom Abraham loved so very much.
He could not do without Isaac!

Abraham would rather
lose all his servants,
and all his animals,
and all his money,
and all his goods,
than lose his beloved son Isaac.

And now the Lord had asked him
to give back to God
his dearest possession on earth:
Isaac, his only son . . .
What would Abraham do?

8. That Could Not Be Right

Why did the LORD
ask Abraham
to kill his son?
Why should his dear son die?
That could not be right!

Would not
the Lord Jesus,
that great Lamb, come by and by?
But if Isaac had to die
it was not possible
that this Child,
the Saviour,
would come.
And if the Saviour
did not come,
nobody
would ever be allowed
to live with the LORD in heaven.
Not even Abraham!

Still, the LORD
had promised
that the Saviour
was going to come.
He was going to belong
to the people
of Abraham and Isaac.

But Abraham had only Isaac.
If Isaac was going to die,
no great nation
would come from him.

Still, the LORD had said
to Abraham that
he was going to be
the father
of many nations.
Abraham
had often looked
at the many stars
that twinkled
in the dark sky.
So many,
so mighty
would his people be!
What the LORD
promises
always happens.
Why, then,
did Isaac,
that one little star,
have to die?

9. Abraham Loved the Lord

Abraham heard the voice of the Lord.
He knew what the Lord asked of him.
No gold and no silver.
No servant
and no animal.
No, the Lord asked
for Isaac, his dear son.
Isaac, his only son.
Yes, Abraham
remembered
the promise of the birth
of the great Lamb.
Later, the Saviour
would be born.
But, if Isaac
was going to die now
that could not happen.
And still . . .
Still Abraham did what the Lord asked of him.
He would give his dearest possession
on earth to the Lord, his God.
That is how much Abraham loved the Lord!

Thy will be done, Thy will alone,
On earth below as round Thy throne.
Thy precepts all are wise and true;
Thy holy will we pray to do.[5]

---

[5] Hymn 47:4a *Book of Praise*

10. The Journey

It was still early in the morning.
Abraham got a donkey ready
and prepared himself
for the journey.
He took wood along too.
Isaac and his two servants
were also ready.
They thought that they
had to help with the sacrifice.
The mother of Isaac did not know
what was going to happen.
Abraham had kept it a secret
from everyone.
Only he knew why
they were going on that journey.

They had to go a long way.
Their journey took three days.
Then they came close
to the mountains
of which the Lord had spoken.
At the foot of a mountain
they stopped.
Abraham knew:
on this mountain
it had to be done.

11. We Will Come Back

"My servants,
you have to stay here
with the donkey,"
commanded Abraham.
"We will go up
on the mountain
and bring the sacrifice
to the Lord and worship Him.
When we are finished
we will come back."

The servants of Abraham did
as he told them.
They took the wood
and laid it on the back of Isaac.
Abraham took the fire
and the knife.
Silently they began
climbing the mountain.
Higher they went;
still higher . . .

The servants saw them disappear.
"Soon they will come back,"
they thought.
But was that true?
Would they really be back soon?
Was not Isaac going to be sacrificed?
How could Abraham have said that?

Ah, Abraham knew the Lord.
He knew that the Lord
was the Almighty One.
And he believed
that the Lord was able
to make Isaac alive again,
even after he died.
In that faith
and in that confidence
he walked beside his son.

12. My Father, Where is the Lamb?

Silently the two of them
walked beside each other.
Abraham saw his son
carrying the wood on his back.
Isaac saw the fire
and the knife.
Suddenly the boy
asked something.
He saw the fire,
the wood, the knife . . .
But where was
the sacrificial animal?
"My father,
where is the lamb?"
asked the boy.
What should Abraham
answer him?
He did not yet want to tell
his son the real answer.
That is why he said,
"My son, God will
provide a lamb.
We will leave
that to Him!"

Silently father and son
walked further.
Higher and still higher they went.
Abraham with the fire
and the knife.
Isaac with the wood.
Until they reached
the top of the mountain.

13. You Are the Lamb!

On the mountain
they built
a kind of a table of stone.
Upon it
they carefully spread
the wood
which Isaac
had carried along.
Then Abraham looked
at his son.
He said something
that sounded strange
and unbelievable.
"Isaac, my son,
you are the lamb!
The Lord wants me
to give you
as a sacrifice to Him.
The Lord has told me this.
This time He did not ask
for an animal but for you.
And I also want
to give you to Him.
For I love the Lord more
than I love you,
even though I also love you
very much, my son."

14. Here I Am, Father!

Isaac looked silently
at his father.
He had heard
the unbelievable words.
What? Did his father
have to sacrifice him?
Was he to be
the sacrificial lamb?
Would he have to be layed
on the wood?
Had the Lord really said that?

Isaac was a strong boy.
He was tall and handsome.
Would he jump away?
Would he flee into the mountains?
Would he quickly run to his mother?
He could run much faster than his father!
What would he do?

"Here I am, Father,"
the boy answered.
"If the Lord has said it,
it must be done."

Isaac also loved
the Lord very much.
He was also willing
to give everything to the Lord.

Even his own life.
And as a lamb he walked
to the table of stone . . .

15. Tied Down

Isaac climbed upon the wood.
How strange all of this was.
Never before had the Lord
asked for such a thing.
But now it was happening.
Look, his father bound his arms
and his legs,
just as if he had been an animal.
In a few more moments
Abraham
would not have his son anymore.
Isaac lay upon the wood.
As a lamb he was silent
and did not open his mouth.
High above him
he saw the blue heavens.
There, above the clouds,
dwells the Lord.
Isaac believed
he was soon going to be
with his heavenly Father.

Then all was ready.
Look, Father Abraham
raised his arm.
He held something in his hand . . .
It was . . . the knife!
Then his arm dropped . . .

16. Abraham! Abraham!

"Abraham! Abraham!"
Listen! A voice called.
Abraham recognized
the voice of the Lord.
For a moment
he held his arm still.
Reverently
he stopped his work,
for it was the Lord
who was speaking.
"Abraham,
do not harm the boy.
I did not want
you to kill the boy.
I only wanted to know
if you were willing
to give your only son to Me.
Now I know
that you love Me
more than anything else!"

Abraham's arm went down.
The knife was held back.
There was no more danger for Isaac.
The boy was allowed to live.

Another came in his place.
Listen! There was a rustling sound . . .

17. Still An Animal

Abraham heard the sound.
He saw the bushes moving.
Then he saw a ram,
a male sheep.
The animal was stuck
by his horns in the shrubs.
It could not move at all.
Listen, how it tried
to get itself free.
Then Abraham understood
that the Lord had supplied
this animal.
It was to be sacrificed
instead of Abraham's son.
Quickly he cut the cords
that bound Isaac to the altar.
Isaac, his son, was now free.
Soon the ram was tied
onto the wood.
Again, the arm of Abraham
was lifted up.
But when the hand
with the knife
went down this time,
no voice was heard.
The ram was killed
and the wood began to burn.

Abraham and Isaac reverently watched the smoke rise up to heaven.

Bind festal off'rings to the altar;
With sacrifices bring Him laud.
Shout forth your joy within His temple.
O praise the LORD, for He is God.[6]

---
[6] Psalm 118:7b *Book of Praise*

18. The Greatest Miracle

The servants saw
Abraham and Isaac
coming back.
And soon they all
were on their way home.
Silently
Abraham and Isaac
walked beside each other.
They remembered
the great promise
of the coming Saviour.
Later, the Lord Jesus
was going to be born.
Oh, that would be wonderful!

The heavenly Father
was going to send His Son
to the earth.
He would give His only Son,
just as Abraham had done.

And the Son, the Lord Jesus
would allow Himself to be bound.
He was willing to die on the cross.
He would give Himself,
just as Isaac had done.

So the Lord Jesus would die.

The great Lamb of God
would die in the place of Abraham
and in the place of Isaac
and in the place of all His children.
Just as the ram had died for Isaac.

That was the greatest miracle.

Yet as the Law must be fulfilled
Or we must die despairing,
Christ Jesus came; God's wrath He stilled,
Our human nature sharing.
The law He has for us obeyed
And thus the Father's vengeance stayed
Which over us impended.[7]

---

[7] Hymn 24:4 *Book of Praise* (based on Romans 5)

Anak, the Eskimo Boy
by Piet Prins

F. Pronk in *The Messenger*: Anak is an Eskimo Boy, who with his family, lives with the rest of their tribe in the far north. The author describes their day-to-day life as they hunt for seals, caribou and walruses. Anak is being prepared to take up his place as an adult and we learn how he is introduced to the tough way of life needed to survive in the harsh northern climate. We also learn how Anak and his father get into contact with the white man's civilization. . . This book makes fascinating reading, teaching about the ways of Eskimos, but also of the power of the Gospel. Anyone over eight years old will enjoy this book and learn from it.

for age 8 - 99   ISBN 0-921100-11-6   Can.$6.95 U.S.$6.30

Tekko Series
by Alie Vogelaar

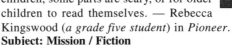

. . . You will watch a little African boy do his utmost to save his little sister. You will see his whole village turn against him. And you will see how God works in wondrous ways to help him. I highly recommend this book for parents to read to their young children, some parts are scary, or for older children to read themselves. — Rebecca Kingswood (*a grade five student*) in *Pioneer*.

Subject: Mission / Fiction   **Age: 8-99**
1 *Tekko and the White Man*
            ISBN 0-921100-47-7 Can.$7.95 U.S.$6.90

2 *Tekko the Fugitive*
            ISBN 0-921100-74-4 Can.$7.95 U.S.$6.90

3 *Tekko Returns*
            ISBN 0-921100-75-2 Can.$7.95 U.S.$6.90

William of Orange - The Silent Prince
by W.G. Van de Hulst

F. Pronk in *The Messenger*: If you have ever wondered why Dutch Reformed people of former generations felt such strong spiritual ties with Dutch royalty, this is a "must" reading. In simple story form, understandable for children ages 10 and up, the Dutch author, wellknown for Christian children's literature, relates the true story of the origin of Dutch royalty. It all began with William of Nassau (1533-1584) . . . He dedicated his life and lost it for the cause of maintaining and promoting Protestantism in the Netherlands.

for age 9 - 99   ISBN 0-921100-15-9 Can.$8.95 U.S.$7.90

Judy's Own Pet Kitten by An Rook

Fay S. Lapka in *Christian Week*: Judy, presumably seven or eight years of age, is the youngest member of a farm family whose rural setting could be anywhere in Canada. The story of Judy, first losing her own kitten, then taming a wild stray cat with kittens, and finally rescuing the tiniest one from a flood, is well-told and compelling.

Subject: Fiction   **Age: 6-10**
ISBN 0-921100-34-5   **Can.$4.95 U.S.$4.50**

Susanneke by C. J. Van Doornik

Little Susanneke is happy! Tomorrow is Christmas. And Daddy has cleaned the church. But did he forget something? When it is her birthday Mommy always decorates the livingroom. And actually they will celebrate the Lord Jesus' birthday tomorrow. But the church isn't decorated at all. Could the big people have forgotten it? That is sad for the Lord. He loves us so much and now no one has thought about decorating the church for Him. She has to think about that for a moment. What should she do?

Subject: Fiction   **Age: 6-8**
ISBN 0-921100-61-2   **Can.$4.95 U.S.$4.50**

Salt in His Blood
The Life of Michael De Ruyter
by William R. Rang

The greatest Dutch Admiral is an example of Christian love and piety, and fascinating because of his many true adventures as a sailer-boy, captain, and pirate-hunter.

Time: 1607 - 1676   **Age: 10-99**
ISBN 0-921100-59-0   **Can.$10.95 U.S.$9.90**

It Began With a Parachute
by William R. Rang

Fay S. Lapka in *Christian Week*: [It] . . . is a well-told tale set in Holland near the end of the Second World War. . . The story, although chock-full of details about life in war-inflicted Holland, remains uncluttered, warm, and compelling.

Time: 1940-1945   **Age: 9-99**
ISBN 0-921100-38-8   **Can.$8.95 U.S.$7.90**

When The Morning Came by Piet Prins
Struggle for Freedom Series 1

D. Engelsma in the *Standard Bearer*: This is reading for Reformed children, young people, and (if I am any indication) their parents. It is the story of 12-year old Martin Meulenberg and his family during the Roman Catholic persecution of the Reformed Christians in the Netherlands about the year 1600. A peddlar, secretly distributing Reformed books from village to village, drops a copy of Guido de Brès' *True Christian Confession* — a booklet forbidden by the Roman Catholic authorities. An evil neighbor sees the book and informs . . .

for age 9 - 99

ISBN 0-921100-12-4   Can.$9.95 U.S.$8.90

Dispelling the Tyranny by Piet Prins
Struggle for Freedom Series 2

"Father! Mother! I saw Count Lodewyk! He rode through the city on a black horse!" Martin shouted, as he dashed into the humble home where his parents were eating supper. "The cavalry followed him, and everywhere he went the people cheered him on!" Martin's eyes sparkled with excitement.

for age 9 - 99

ISBN 0-921100-40-X   Can.$9.95 U.S.$8.90

Augustine, The Farmer's Boy of Tagaste
by P. De Zeeuw

C. MacDonald in *The Banner of Truth*: Augustine was one of the great teachers of the Christian Church, defending it against many heretics. This interesting publication should stimulate and motivate all readers to extend their knowledge of Augustine and his works.

J. Sawyer in *Trowel & Sword*: . . . It is informative, accurate historically and theologically, and very readable. My daughter loved it (and I enjoyed it myself). An excellent choice for home and church libraries.

Time: 354 - 430 A.D.   Age: 9-99
ISBN 0-921100-05-1   Can.$7.95 U.S.$6.90

The Escape by A. Van der Jagt
The Adventures of Three Huguenot Children Fleeing Persecution

F. Pronk in *The Messenger*: This book . . . will hold its readers spellbound from beginning to end. The setting is late seventeenth century France. Early in the story the mother dies and the father is banished to be a galley slave for life on a war ship. Yet in spite of threats and punishment, sixteen-year-old John and his ten-year-old sister Manette, refuse to give up the faith they have been taught.

Time: 1685 - 1695 **Age: 12-99**
ISBN 0-921100-04-3 **Can.$11.95 U.S.$9.95**

The Secret Mission by A. Van der Jagt
A Huguenot's Dangerous Adventures in the Land of Persecution

In the sequel to our best-seller, *The Escape,* John returns to France with a secret mission of the Dutch Government. At the same time he attempts to find his father.

Time: 1702-1712 **Age: 12-99**
ISBN 0-921100-18-3 **Can.$14.95 U.S.$10.95**

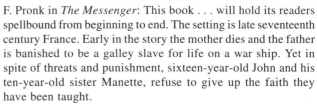
How They Kept The Faith by Grace Raymond
A Tale of the Huguenots of Languedoc

Eglantine and Rene grew up together in a Huguenot family. Already at a young age they are committed to become each other's life's partner. When persecution breaks out they each must endure their individual struggles to remain faithful to God and to each other. A must for teenagers and adults.

Time: 1676 - 1686 **Age: 13-99**
ISBN 0-921100-64-7 **Can.$14.95 U.S.$12.90**

The Young Huguenots by Edith S. Floyer

It was a happy life at the pretty chateau. Even after that dreadful Sunday evening, when strange men came down and shut the people out of the church not much changed for the four children. Until the soldiers came . . .

Time: 1686 - 1687 **Age: 11-99**
ISBN 0-921100-65-5 **Can.$11.95 U.S.$9.90**

Abide With Me (Instrumental Hymns)
Noortje Van Middelkoop, Panflute
Harm Hoeve, Organ
Anja Van Der Maten, Oboe; Edith & Arjan Post, Trumpets; Hendrie Westra, Xylophone

C. Van Dam in *Clarion*: This CD of instrumental hymns will quickly become a family favourite. The music is of a very high quality and the selections played are bound to have a wide appeal (e.g., Genevan, traditional and more modern hymns, as well as some classical such as Handel, Purcell and Mozart). The sensitive opening solo selection, "Abide With Me", by Noortje Van Middelkoop on the panflute is superb and sets the right tone (pardon the pun) for what follows. Together with Harm Hoeve on the organ, this duet brings to new life and vigour tunes one may not have been aware had such potential for sparkle and appeal. Some of the selections also involve Anja Van Der Maten playing the oboe, Edith and Arjan Post with trumpets and Hendrie Westra on the xylophone. All in all a very delightful and uplifting recording which I hope will be enjoyed by many in our midst. In an age of much trash music, a CD such as this needs to be heard in our families. May it also be used to build appreciation for good music.

Abide With Me (*Eventide*); I Love The Lord (*Genevan 116*); As a Deer Pants For the Water; Praise the Lord With Drums and Cymbals; With All My Heart (*Genevan 138*); All Through the Night (*Old Welsh Air*); Interludium: Prelude in Classic Style; I Need Thee Every Hour (*Need*); Our Faithful God Makes Plans (*Gregor's 112th Metre*); Abba Father; Alleluia; Yerushala im Shel Zahav; Trumpet Voluntary; Greensleeves; Great is Thy Faithfulness (*Faithfulness*); The Lord's My Shepherd (*Crimond*); There is a Redeemer; Praise Be To The Lord (*Rule Britannia*); Abide With Me (*Eventide*).

Compact Disc CMR 106-2   **Can.$21.99 U.S.$18.99**
Cassette 106-4   **Can.$14.99 U.S.$12.99**

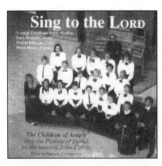

Sing to the LORD
The Children of Asaph sing the Psalms of David on the tunes of John Calvin — Noortje Van Middelkoop, Panflute; Lucy Bootsma, Violin; Daniel Bootsma, Cello; Harm Hoeve, Organ; Theresa Janssen, Conductor.

Byron Snapp in *The Counsel of Chalcedon*: ... There is a richness and depth in these selections that is too often missing in much contemporary music... Once again *Church Music & Records* has provided the listener with the opportunity to hear enduring Psalms sung and played with meaning and a quiet, sure confidence. Hopefully this recording will be widely purchased and used in the lives of many for the building up of God's people more and more unto His glory.

1. Psalm 42:1, 2, & 5 *Willem Van Twillert*; 2. Psalm 116:1, 2, 3, & 7 *Theresa E. Janssen*; 3. Psalm 124 *Harm Hoeve*; 4. Psalm 1 (Organ Solo) *Feike Asma*; 5. Psalm 49:1 & 2 (solo: Hester Barendregt) *Willem Van Twillert*; 6. Psalm 98 (solo: Cynthia Van Leeuwen & Karina Van Laar) *Trad./Harm Hoeve;* 7. Psalm 121 *Feike Asma*; 8. Psalm 96:1, 2, & 8 *Dick Van Luttikhuizen*; 9. Psalm 80:1, 2, & 3 (solo: Felicia Amy Barendregt) *Roelof A. Janssen*; 10. Psalm 68 (Organ & Panflute) *Peter Eilander*; 11. Psalm 25:1, 2, & 3 *Willem Hendrik Zwart*; 12. Song of Simeon (Hymn 18) *Feike Asma*; 13. Psalm 134 *Harm Hoeve/Klaas Jan Mulder*.   For all ages!

Compact Disc CMR 104-2   **Can.$21.99 U.S.$18.99**
Cassette CMR 104-4   **Can.$14.99 U.S.$12.99**